AF270621

Griffins

by Grace Hansen

Abdo Kids Jumbo is an Imprint of Abdo Kids
abdobooks.com

abdobooks.com

Published by Abdo Kids, a division of ABDO, P.O. Box 398166, Minneapolis, Minnesota 55439.
Copyright © 2024 by Abdo Consulting Group, Inc. International copyrights reserved in all countries.
No part of this book may be reproduced in any form without written permission from the publisher.
Abdo Kids Jumbo™ is a trademark and logo of Abdo Kids.

Printed in the United States of America, North Mankato, Minnesota.

102023

012024

Photo Credits: AdobeStock, Alamy, Getty Images, Granger Collection, Shutterstock,
©User:moon knight p22/CC BY-SA 4.0

Production Contributors: Teddy Borth, Jennie Forsberg, Grace Hansen
Design Contributors: Candice Keimig, Pakou Moua

Library of Congress Control Number: 2023937696
Publisher's Cataloging-in-Publication Data

Names: Hansen, Grace, author.

Title: Griffins / by Grace Hansen

Description: Minneapolis, Minnesota : Abdo Kids, 2024 | Series: World of mythical beings | Includes online
    resources and index.

Identifiers: ISBN 9781098268602 (lib. bdg.) | ISBN 9781098269302 (ebook) | ISBN 9781098269654
    (Read-to-Me ebook)

Subjects: LCSH: Griffins--Juvenile literature. | Mythical animals--Juvenile literature. | Folklore--Juvenile
    literature. | Legends--Juvenile literature.

Classification: DDC 398.2454--dc23

Table of Contents

The Myth of the Griffin 4

Early Griffins. 8

Griffins throughout the World . . 12

Griffins Today. 20

More Hybrid Creatures 22

Glossary 23

Index 24

Abdo Kids Code. 24

The Myth of the Griffin

Griffins are legendary creatures. They have the body, tail, and back legs of a lion. They have the head, wings, and front legs of an eagle.

Both lions and eagles are

powerful animals. This made

the Griffin the ruler of the

land and air.

Early Griffins

Images of Griffins have been around for thousands of years. They first appeared as early as 4000 BCE in **Mesopotamia**.

9

By the 14th century BCE,
the legend of the Griffin had
spread. Stories were especially
popular in western Asia and
Greece.

Griffins throughout the World

The ancient Egyptians showed the griffin with a **feline** body. It had the head of a falcon. Griffins are shown in art from Egypt and other **cultures** pulling the chariots of rulers.

PERVSIN
13

In Greek mythology, Griffins pulled Apollo's chariot across the sky. They were the only animal worthy of the task. They were also said to be companions and protectors of Zeus.

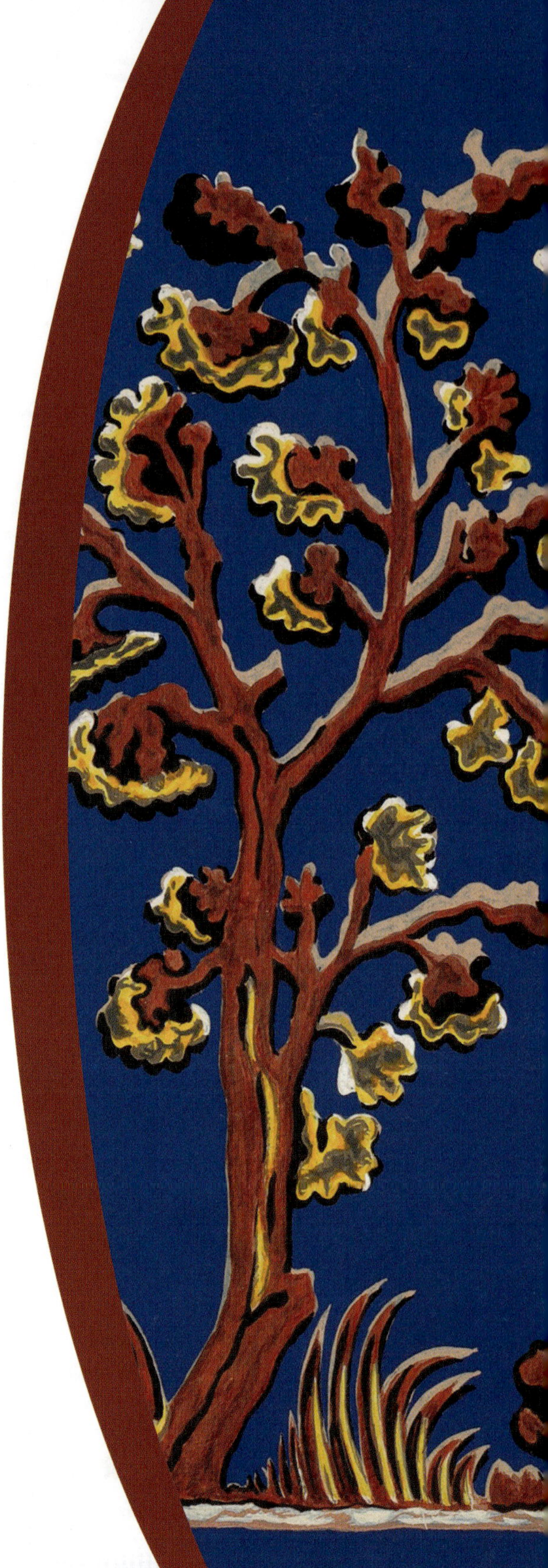

15

The ancient Greeks believed
Griffins lived at the edge of the
world. They described Griffins as
fierce and powerful creatures.

Both Herodotus and Pliny the

Elder wrote about Griffins.

They said that the creatures

guarded large amounts of gold.

People began to see Griffins as

protectors of treasure and people.

Griffins Today

Today, Griffins are still known as noble protectors. Griffins appear on company logos, on coats of arms, and as school mascots. They are also in many fantasy fiction books and movies.

More Hybrid Creatures

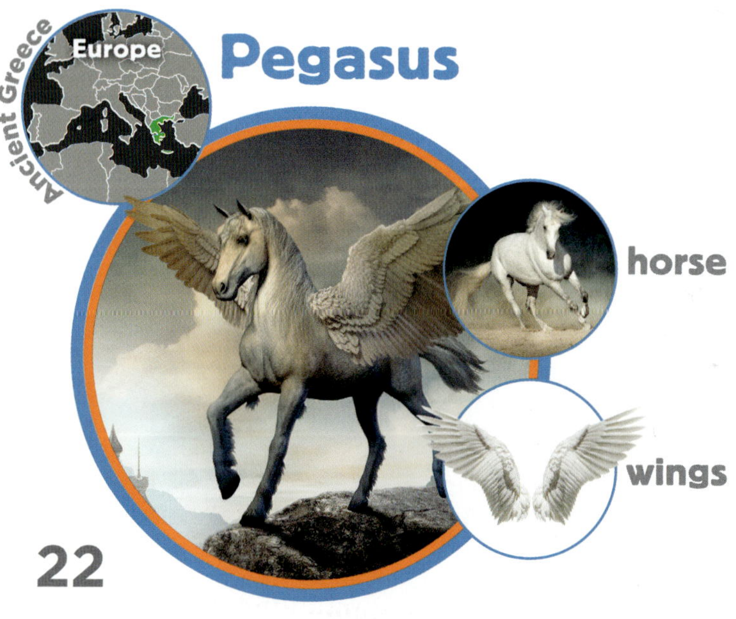

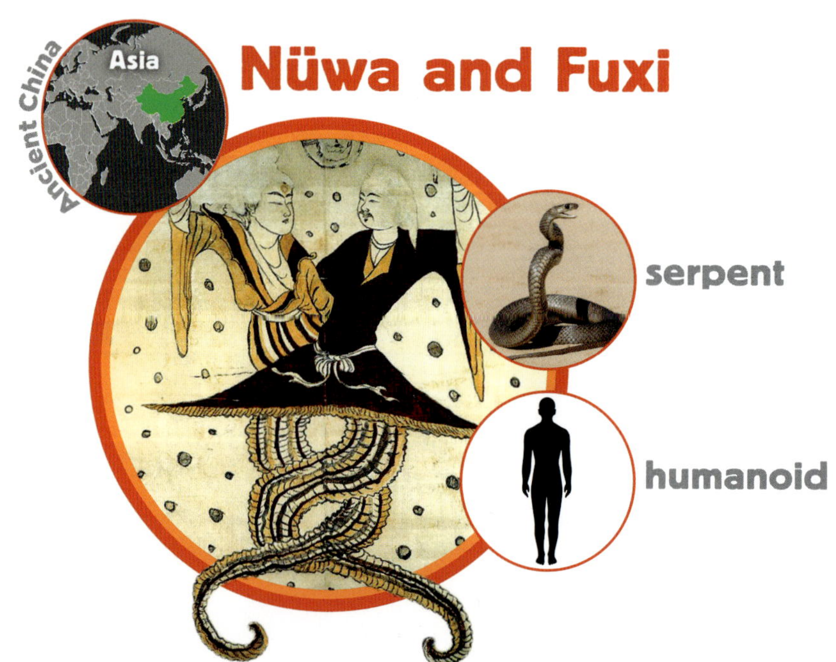

Glossary

culture – the language, customs, ideas, and art of a particular group of people.

fantasy fiction – a type of story or literature that is set in a magical world.

feline – a closely related group of animals that includes both large cats (lions or tigers) and small cats (house cats or bobcats).

fierce – violently hostile or aggressive in temperament.

Mesopotamia – a historical region of West Asia that was the site of several ancient civilizations.

noble – of or showing a strong or excellent mind or character.

Index

Apollo 14

appearance 4, 12

Asia 10

Egypt 12

Greece 10, 14, 16

Greek mythology 14, 16

Herodotus 18

media 20

Mesopotamia 8

Pliny the Elder 18

protector 14, 18, 20

treasure 18

Zeus 14

Abdo Kids
ONLINE
FREE! ONLINE MULTIMEDIA RESOURCES

Visit **abdokids.com** to access crafts, games, videos, and more!

Use Abdo Kids code **WGK8602** or scan this QR code!